RADIOACTIVE WOLVES

AMY ROA

POETRY

STEEL TOE BOOKS
est. 2003

ISBN 978-1-949540-37-6

Steel Toe Books
steeltoebooks.com

For special discounted bulk purchases, please contact sales@steeltoebooks.com

RADIOACTIVE WOLVES

CONTENTS

For Keith

Axolotl

I never got really good at building heavily armored beasts.
The shape of the wrists
always unfurled,
headed somewhere else
where the butter supply was plentiful.
The axolotl suited me better.
There's no word to describe the joy of putting an axolotl in the sky.
I shot one out of a cannon in an attempt to help him evolve wings.
"Adapt or die," I whispered and lit the match.
There was plenty of room up there.
He soared above the yellow grass,
above pelicans with rotten bills and stringy, matted feathers.
Someday he'll turn up again, I thought. Unless, of course, he
freezes to death like the dinosaurs.
But there was no freeze, I corrected myself.
There were those who kept to themselves, bounded forward with
eager steps
to make nests near shimmering surfaces
and listen to echoes bouncing off the bodies of insects.
Though, it's true they left no written account of their peace or war.
If you trace back the origins of the axolotl,
you end up at the point in history
where they fail to conquer the sky.
I shoved another axolotl into a cannon,
looked to the right side of her face, where all the clues are laid out,
assured her that a star is the closest thing to a perfect black body.

Moth

The platypuses formed a colony near the overhead power lines.
How could I forget?
That colony glowed an incandescent red
like a car on fire.
What's more, another of my grandfather's mistresses could make
seventeen different facial expressions when snorting cocaine
and she called the creatures prophets.
Among young people, this was the best place to squeeze into a
crack in a wall and try to communicate with another species.
I'd chosen the moth, though platypuses were plentiful.
What a brain I had! Brown-colored and bigger than an elephant's,
more than enough to run my body metabolically.
I thought the prettiest thoughts. Think of sawing a robot in half,
I'd tell myself.
Adding debris between the empty spaces in its gears
and after a prolonged confrontation with mirrors,
it learns to recognize its own image looking back.
If my grandfather's mistress passed away from cirrhosis of the
liver, I can't say,
but her heart swirled and accelerated into a new continent.
She'd found her way through grief to fall in love with the teenage
boy who was said to have talked to Jesus, laughed with Jesus,
whacked Jesus with a skateboard
and brought him to his knees.
And there was no problem recognizing the hierarchy of moth
communication.
When a moth flies at a bright light,
again and again the history of its origin is written in its own book
of the dead.
I clicked my nails and said I want to have a look at them, the size
of them
moving toward a flame.

The functioning of a moth nervous system as it learns a language,
keeps the beats of the wings
separate and unassembled,
knows that a space exists
where the light parts itself in half
and tumbles down into the sagebrush to feed on salamanders.

Animal Kingdom

The first finback whale took an evolutionary leap onto land,
and the president was on TV,
shaking the whale's fin,
all sleek and blubber.
All that was on a Tuesday.
On Wednesday, my parents adopted a small,
elderly man to be my little brother.
They set him up on a high chair and wrapped their arms around
him.
He bowed his bald head and gurgled with joy.
My new brother ate all the meat in the freezer
and often swatted the flies in his room at night,
leaving his dead all over the floor.
I came home from school every day
and sat next to him.
I told him all the new things I'd learned.
I said, "The finback whale's finally balanced on its new legs
and dances with wealthy women.
It wants to buy a gun, big like a house."
My new brother swayed his body back and forth like an ocean,
remembering when, ages ago,
we swum beneath ice sheets,
before we too
descended from the animal kingdom.

Cherries

Last Tuesday, Jennifer M. accidentally left her aquarium plenty with electric catfish in a hot August car. There was nothing living in the aquarium after that. She'd taken the bodies of her friends to the mermaids by the maraschino cherry factory. In urban settings like these, you often came in contact with mermaids flopping on land, grooming one another's hair.

She said they'd looked sickly and pale. "It's all that alcohol and maraschino juice that they drink," she said. "They probably miss being weightless," she pointed out.

The mermaids lifted old bicycle chains above their heads and muttered a few words in their language. They turned the dead catfish into live creatures that run on four toes on the front feet and three on the hind feet.

One of the electric catfish developed a mammalian heart. He flared his gills and there seemed to be some kind of war in him.

He took a magic marker out of Jennifer M.'s backpack, drawing large so everything could be seen, drew the empty spaces in the galaxies. "No telling what's over there," the mermaids said in English. They offered the catfish a handful of maraschino cherries. He ate heartily.

Jennifer M.'s said that he'd moved about in the most beautiful way, he'd cast an electric shadow,

emitted an electric pulse,
an electric pattern like a song of love.

Minotaur

We were fifth graders.

Ms. Hurley had invited the Minotaur to display his vast collection to the class. He dressed formally in shined shoes, held up in a glass case

a skinless muscle.

He said, "This was the heart when she was married."

He didn't explain who she was, or why only her heart remained.

"The architecture of the body. The deepest layers," he went on. We were in awe. Dion asked if he hunted at dusk.

"Only if it's snowing."

Ms. Hurley passed out paints and permanent markers. The Minotaur invited us to decorate the swallowed stones inside the alligator stomach.

"He was large, hard to take down," the Minotaur said. "But it's impossible to really know oneself."

I slumped over my desk to rest my head in my arms and listened as the Minotaur's tail whacked something on the tiled floor. On my swallowed stone, I painted the weather inside a zebra stripe. I generated its lightning, the blankets of pulverized ice. It was a place you'd never want to return to. While the paint still dried, the Minotaur reached over and grabbed the stone with his hooves.

"Generous use of color," he said. His voice trembled. He brought the stone to his nostrils. Detected its smell, its warmth, shed one slow-moving tear.

"I had a pony like this once," he said.

Mermaid

It was a terrain of TV satellite dishes as far as the eye could see.
Every rat was well fed,
and men of all ages flooded into the parks at night and were struck
deaf.
Shortly thereafter, they disappeared into the bone-dry earth.
That is the way of things, people disappear every day.
Besides, there are other things to worry about.
Several theories still persist as to why there's an iridescent strip
of plasma living 90 degrees above our heads, and why neurons
explode on a particular spot near the sun's magnetic field.
Honestly, I never thought of such things.
I had grown up around nocturnal ambush predators.
I stole bottles of liquor and threw the empties off of rooftops
where we used to sleep.
"We're just like the birds," I'd say.
One time, I even held down a job feeding buckets of fish to the
mermaids by the pier.
Beto lived nearby and removed his left lung on command,
showed it off in his palm, then displayed it in the middle of his
table like a cake of fig leaves.
It was a soft, gleaming thing,
prettier than that emerald we once found engulfed in the back of
a mermaid's throat.
We sprung backward when she lunged to poke deep holes in our
abdomens.
But what I remember most,
mermaids circling the discarded potatoes
and plastic flamingos
floating in high tide,
oxygen suspended inside the walls of a lung,
air exhaling,
embracing itself.

Stories

My best friend at the time was a bull shark I'd dragged home
after a hurricane deposited him in the middle of the road.
"You've got a heart like a seal," he'd said, then opened his jaws to
reveal a cluster of birds.
He hadn't yet warmed to human company, but the bull shark and
I never got into any fights.
There were huge factories and an ocean
dotting our perimeter.
Maybe you've dunked both arms in the water after bombers set
fire to a city,
or went on a field trip
where there, on the ground, you saw the flesh within birds,
but you've never heard this story.
Or the one where I sleep in the shade of a house
and dream of the swollen necks of mango trees.
I created that place to live from photographs I'd seen. Talk about
irresponsible,
I made the sea level exceptionally low,
and the jellyfish move along the carpet,
though we're never in the same room together.
All the lights are out and reincarnated dogs run through the hallway,
they grip their bodies and cradle themselves,
swatting mosquitoes away with their tails.

Job

Especially since I'd looked down an elephant's throat
and seen the gamma rays streaming out
outshining everything,
I thought of becoming a gamma ray myself.
But I'd felt underfed for weeks,
and got sidetracked eating pinecones.
The only job left for me was as a grain of rainforest soil,
a casted bit of sediment by the sharp bend that brings the river full
circle.
I had a going away party.
I gloated to everyone that I'd never have to make plans again,
"No more worrying about empty cereal boxes," I said.
There were subtle modifications over time.
First, I saw tails of all different sizes.
Here and there, an ant was being executed.
I lived with a current of wind, "I like you because you're honest,"
I said.
But soon it had to retreat to a different territory.
We hugged one another,
and I made landfall on the scales of a mermaid as it sunned itself
on a rock.
I spoke in its dialect.
I spoke of the hours of night and day,
of the happiness of tree rings.
"I'm not always sad," the mermaid said.
It liked watching suicidal men,
the ones who would put a knife to their own throats
or lay hands inside a fire's mouth.
It called to them,
a whine,
a buzzing sound,
translated meant, come closer and like my face.

Winged Insects

We formed a human chain to rescue a family caught in a rip current.
We were miles away from everything.
Mary Ortega's white and tan dog walked along the shore, his paws
right above a fault line
where metals twist and drive rocks into empty corners.
He sat there and watched us and wept like a human,
the way my uncle Mingo wept
when he accidentally fired a nail gun
into a spot in his heart.
When he came to, he explained that the whole process was like
watching an older model of yourself carrying a family of tawny
goats on your shoulders. He was just happy his mustache was still
intact.

We walked home across the highway, not saying a word. There
was so much sky above us and we were all homesick. Our English
teacher, Mr. Samuels, drove by in his Toyota and stopped to ask
Jennifer M. if she wanted a ride home. He thought about Jennifer
M. without her shirt on. He thought about her hands on his chest.

We roared like the crazy lady on Rogers Avenue who kept her
freezer full of dead kittens. We had no clue then that Mr. Samuels
would die the next Saturday. He'd be killed by a criminal who had
a wife. The wife kept her face soft and liked to talk to him about
love.

Toward the end of the day, a streetlight at the edge of a sidewalk
drew dozens of winged insects. They rested on the spot where the
surface was warmest.
I pointed up at them and said, "As you get closer to the middle,
everything there becomes edible, everything there has a life."

Ghost Heart

The unicorn is out looking for a ghost heart.
Well, not really a ghost heart,
but a translucent pig heart with all the living cells washed away.
Only the protein structure remains.
Just glancing at one is known to erase the wrinkles above nostrils.
A Florida woman paid the unicorn good money for the ghost heart.
You wouldn't think unicorns placed any importance on money,
but even they need adult braces and fancy gilt picture frames.
I witnessed the richest unicorn chewing the heads off of hundred-dollar bills
as the space shuttle launched
on its way to mine minerals on one of Jupiter's moons.

The Food Chain

"This is what happens when the world ends," my mother said.
Her own father had been killed by sentient robots in a Volkswagen
factory when she was a girl, so she felt she knew something about
loss.
The night robots killed her father,
birds burrowed into the hearts of banana trees,
compromising their immune systems,
the woman next door suckled a newborn goat after her baby died
from parasites,
and the jaguars hiding in the bushes
ate four humans in one night.
"And that's just the food chain," my mother said.
The mosquitoes gathered under the dark sky breaking open and
spilling,
and my mother wept for her father.
"He'd developed one of the longest fasting periods of any
vertebrate animal in history.
Scientists would have studied him like they'd study a dolphin tail
grown in a lab."
She often complained of the heat blistering the backs of her knees
and of the noise made by the conjoined twin brothers
living in the apartment above.
Once, I heard them burst into laughter,
"I can see right through your internal organs," one or both of them
said.

Queen

The smallest species of sheep had evolved in the tropical ecosystem
of the Dominican Republic.
Like most quadrupeds of the time, they had one set of teeth to last
a lifetime,
holes in the lining of their ear drums, eyes that burned some
afternoons, and seemed to have a bird's crucial feather floating
around in their brains.
A herd of them living on a patch of wild lawn on the shore of Boca
Chica beach.
Between the green blades of grass,
the miniature sheep grazed throughout the day.
They were no bigger than ants. I squatted down and fed them bits
of a discarded mango.
I liked watching them cart away bits of the flesh. I liked their black
and white hair.
I kept the seagulls away from them.
They walked up my arm in a line, baying all the way.
I carried them out to the edge of the ocean.
A few of the lambs confused the roar and the splash of the waves
for the beat of their own hearts. The others listened to the sound
of my voice reach down into the deep until it struck the lost black
boxes of fallen airplanes.
They listened carefully, and I wondered if they'd developed a
fondness for me,
if one day they'd place a crown of giant lilies on my head,
bow down on two hooves,
call me their queen.

Biologies

A professor and a doctor walk onto a farm to measure the mechanical pressure and heat
surrounding the inflated carcass of a cloud decomposing on the ground by a tractor.
From time to time, they can make out the giant face of a wolf cub within the tiny water droplets of the body. The professor holds the cloud.
He says, "What a slow-moving creature it must have been. Fewer than two generations ago, he probably had soft organs like a zebra."
The doctor, frightened now of the silence, wills the sparrow stapled to his aorta to flutter its wings and sing.
He tells the professor, "Growing up, I never wanted to be a doctor, I wanted to be a small table built for snails where they might dine on dandelion greens."
The professor nods along and says, "Funny how life never turns out the way you want it." Then he records the time it takes for the edges of the cloud to break apart, for the wolf cub's nose to migrate to the top of its head.
Down the road at the farmhouse, the farmer's wife calls them over to drink from the garden hose, her belly 8 months full of baby.
"It's a boy," she says, "his little ribs are made out of raccoon bones."

Mollusk

I was far away from home and on my way to see our mother's
reincarnated soul
ushered into the body of a newly born three-legged girl
living somewhere in the sugarcane fields.
When I tell that story,
sometimes I mention that our mother didn't know anyone who
didn't like the taste of beef,
that for years she had us living in a house that flooded in hurricane
season.
And although our eldest brother was going blind from cataracts,
he caught fish in the living room with palm leaves.
He was the kindest one of us all.
He'd feed sugar water to the moths on the window
and say, "Evening is upon us like the mountains."
We had no inherited memories.
We were nothing like our mother,
who remembered all her lives,
like the one where her lungs burst out of their scars into tree roots
crawled up to touch the ceiling,
or the ancient mollusk that she once was,
drifting through Earth's shallow oceans
for more than two hundred million years,
her fossilized shells washing up all over the world.

Flood

The anatomy of a giant Pacific octopus was there at the beginning.
The three hearts, blue blood, and the nine brains hunting for
lobsters
while the moon's gravitational pull,
the maker of planetary tides,
caused a cluster of high tide floods.
The tides flooded the cities, towns, forests, and the airport
with the chimpanzees living on the beams inside the ceilings,
they really didn't want to leave.
The airport had become an island that was there or wasn't there,
depending on the tide.
Aircraft tires were overgrown with green seaweed and razor clams,
moon snails translucent when a chimpanzee held them up to the
sun.
They signed to each other the words they'd been taught at the
Yerkes Primate Research Center. They put two known words
together,
referred to the giant Pacific octopus in terminal B as the arm fish.
A movement of the arm fish's eight arms through the surface,
and one of the older female chimpanzees stopped smashing the
tortoise shell against the luggage carousel, left the tortoise meat
untouched,
rocked her body forward and back.
A younger female approached,
proceeded to pluck the splinters off the older female's hair,
placed a hand on the other's rib cage,
an open wound there
drilled ages ago by scientists studying infections of the primate
lung.
The older female showed her teeth,
spiraled the words she'd learned from her black lungs into her
hands,
"Help me," she signed. "It hurts."

The Pulmonary System

Like everyone interested in the pulmonary system,
I studied the eating habits of the Bombay night frog.
Whether lost on a windswept road or studying a reflection in a
bathroom mirror,
they swallow flies in the landscape,
their lungs stretch 260 feet at the widest point.
What a shock it must have been,
everything buckling under its own weight.
In the darkness
entire abdomens vibrate.
You'd think they suffered from chronic tuberculosis.
It was nice there for a minute,
a chorus of Bombay night frogs singing in the elevator shafts,
and all us kids from the pool,
we looked like any other tribe watching the climate crawl out of
the cells of moss perfectly.
We took pleasure in the views from our homes
and in the gap in a tree canopy above.
The leaves curled down and touched the elbows of my babysitter,
Yvonne.
She sunbathed under the branches and fed me a diet of canned
pineapple.
She often dreamt that the famous star of film and television,
Danny Glover, was her father.
Her boyfriend had killed her real father several weeks before.
Together they'd stolen the money he'd hidden away in a shoe
box.
"In any case, I'll never do that again," she said, and swung me up
by the legs, flopped me on the grass like fresh-caught squid.
She said, "If you're lucky, one day your brain will grow through
a crack in your nose. You'll be smart enough to find all the finest
horses and ponies."
Later that day, I turned nine and was bit by a scorpion on a train

heading upstate.
The tilt of the Earth
caused the woman sitting next me to grow feathers all over her
body.
She pinned back her ears, narrowed her eyes, took off flying
through the train car.
In the middle of all this, experts have been saying for years we're
mostly composed of water. We'll move across the world
as a boat or a glacier
and our skin will tan well.
Why, even the dogs will have a good time.

Everything #1

There's a story about the old dictator. It goes: He climbed up a ladder and found a black hole at the top.
He roared with agony.
Meanwhile, the black hole struggled to comprehend its own life.

It's bad luck to look in the face of a mongoose.
Mongooses follow your scent for long hours.
When they find you, they lick your head and leave a ribbon of white limestone halfway up your skull.

Soon it was my dog, Laika, who looked up startled.
She'd never seen such a night.
She liked to eat singing frogs in the dark.

It was my turn to wear the gas mask.
Yamilis said, "You look like an extraterrestrial."
It was true. I'd been in orbit for five months. My capsule plunged into the atmosphere, burned up over the Caribbean.
I showed my claws. "I'm strong, but I'm afraid of stoves," I told her.
"Hold this stone. Hold it like a pet," she said.
It was a meteor heavy in my arms.
"I'll be so good to it," I said.

You wouldn't believe the island I found built on empty clam shells.
Horses stand there all evening.

Our grandfather gifted us each a rifle.
He said, "Columbus took one look at us and said we'd make good servants."
We stood under lime trees with rifles, then someone took a photograph.

I tried to think of things besides the flies taking up considerable floor space at my grandmother's feet.

I fell asleep at the table.
The chickens in the yard went silent.

I put clothes on a papaya,
turned it into a man overjoyed that all zombies had been beheaded.

Elisa kept bringing babies home.

The old dictator made scientists dance in red-hot iron shoes.

Laika had ears the length of her body. They flashed a phosphorescent green when she had an itch. She leaned her head against my thigh and glowed when I scratched.

The flies curled up all cozy in the empty belly of an abandoned television.
I thought of things I could burn.

Yamilis' hair grew and grew past her feet, onto the floor, then stretched for at least a mile into the Olympic Stadium. She'd grow up to make wigs for money.

The horses had been rewilded.
Though I was unwell and my face had an unhealthy color, I trotted at their heels.
Our play was all motor activity.
I pushed and tackled
and growled.

The mongoose sat on a chair,
on a spot where the wood had cracked.
She placed a lizard tail on the table and held her body so still, lost herself in herself.

Our grandfather counted the clouds and localized the sound of the hurricane before it coiled us around it like a rope.

All the papayas were people now.
Some were in desperate need of insulin,
some carried succulents like yucca flowers in baskets,
some had arms curving out from a bright center.

I set the chickens free to wander the capital.
They ended up on a small bed in a boarding house, a mosquito net surrounding them.
The same problems followed to that foreign place.

Elisa married a new man and left the babies. She found work at a

makeup counter.
She drew handsome pearl divers
on women's cheeks.
None of the women minded.
They had a history of hunger
for beautiful things.

River

Those white girls in swimsuits,
over by where the sphere of old stars overturned on the narrow
path leading to the Bronx River,
gave me pills for the first time.
Actually, it wasn't pills,
it was a gorgeous horse eye they'd found in the water.
It's a beautiful organ, they'd said,
an iris shaped like a lightbulb.
Then one of them kissed a live, flopping catfish and said it was
her husband now.
I dove into the river head first. I'll be a lamp one day, I thought,
or a flame
with a light's wingspan flickering 7.6 times per second
over trees in full fruit or maybe be swallowed whole
by a gator mouth and all its bones.
How does it all start?
The harsh, low frequency call,
the alarm to the species.
Depending on the season, my hair grows out in two long braids,
two vines grabbing hold of breathing things,
even a living home.
Drag it down,
windows and all, into the river's mud here to stay,
to make words never spoken in its life cycle.

Girls

From the spot where girls had peeled electrical wire out of the walls and wrapped it around their shoulders like cloaks, stood the clone of the long-deceased military leader, Napoleon.

That new Napoleon wouldn't look you in the eye or attack prey.

"They killed the elk and they didn't let me see it," he said, tears streaming down his face.

Those girls just laughed and went back to locating precious stones by sound.

In the suburbs of New York on Valentine's Day, other girls explain the connection between the nervous system and the muscles developed for a life in trees.

They want a Napoleon clone of their very own.

To sit him at the edge of a dam and cover him in lace.

They said, "He'd be just like a baby we could throw into a bouncy castle."

Those girls, their fathers had been sent to prison for the murder of grain dealers.

They know the day sends a pulse of radio waves through the burnt-out shells of cars.

It's as if life in its truest form were elsewhere,

sitting under the asbestos in the crawl space where one girl spits out sunflower seed shells.

She'd just carried a slain deer through the abandoned lot, kicked up her heels like a show pony the whole way.

The weather was just like this,

driving wild things back into the night.

Blades of grass biting the ankles, then wind-borne seeds colonizing the slopes of a recently erupted volcano

while girls twisted their bodies to stop fragments of glass from burying their town.

Then I grew ashamed of myself for not helping them,

for staying home and throwing roasted chestnuts down to the hungry girl stuck in a well.

Her voice reached up and said, "What they don't understand is that if you stay on land too long, you become human."

Bad News

In some unknown place, an old-world monkey controls a robot
with his mind,
and on a warm, sunny Wednesday,
three deer burst into a convenience store and eat everything in
sight.
I could measure their skulls from antler to jaw,
or pass through the arms of the Milky Way only to be bound to
this plot of soil.
It's impossible to predict what would be best.
Soon I won't care about the murder of Venezuelan beauty queens
and forget about the deepest places in the world.
I've been having severe stomach aches for years,
but all the CT scan says is that I've swallowed a cloud,
a heavy thing too big to wrap your jacket around or feed to a goat.
And another thing, heat from the Earth's core continues rising.
Even as other insects have been able to expand their range into
cooler climates,
bumblebees are still stuck in the south,
flying over each other's backs into a dirty white sky.
Outside, meteorologists run through the streets naked.
They say a storm has carried away all their cells,
washed them down a cave, then spouted them back up,
glittering,
encrusted with everything they've ever longed for.

Beasts

He said, "The rule of being eaten by wild animals is to pass through undigested."

He'd lived for centuries. One of his brothers died in the eruption of Pompeii.

"Just think of the work it takes," he said. "Suddenly lava cranks the body up like a machine."

He invited us over one afternoon to sit at his table and watch a fly move around a lightbulb.

"King of all beasts" he called it.

His wife embraced us like children of the house.

She'd wandered out of a marsh at sixteen.

Her eyes still darted about looking for a screen of mangroves or a lost sinkhole.

We toasted to her health. None of us wanted to go home.

His wife's name was Brigida.

Jupiter

They found the fossilized remains of ancient humans on Jupiter.

Half-forgotten things

with ice teeth.

Experts suspect they'd breathed heavily on tree branches until bark reached out embraced their heads, trapping them

into cold wood attuned to the comforts of nature.

There've been other moments in time I could have started all this, but I'll begin here, then move on to when the rats were most active on Jupiter's 71st moon.

They'd seized control of most of the southern territory. Elephants lived along there. They did nothing but roam the streets, sleep in alleyways, and eat garbage.

I played with those elephants, and the magpie with the injury to his leg joined us. We repeated the same games over and over again.

At the end, I dropped dingy carrots at our feet and we took turns eating.

I was really very happy.

The magpie told us about the time he got lost in a hall of mirrors, tapped on every surface and felt his bill become infinite.

The elephants placed their trunks on a hollow log feeling for the lines that define the borders between them and the roots beneath.

The lines, I tell them, are dynamited piles of broken things, full of muscles, prettier than that boy who'd fed on a poisonous cow

then no longer moved.

I thought the magpie should have married him. Together they would have settled on the oddly dimming star over Orion's shoulder.

That star, broken into spontaneous celebration,
pulsed its surface
of convective cells
waggled in a dance of dust clouds.

White Rainbow

The army held the baby in chains. It broke free. It was quite easy. At 158 feet high, it towered over the army and its tanks. It tore the metal wrapped around its wrists and legs with its eight baby teeth.

The baby wobbled toward the freight train yard, as it liked trains, liked the sounds made by trains.

Dion sat against the wire fence by the train yard. He liked reading to the sounds of trains. He liked to read books about the evolution of canid brains. On the afternoon he met the baby, he'd been reading a story about a girl raised by eastern coyotes. Her coyote brothers and sisters tackled her, slammed their bodies into her hips, and licked her face before biting her ears. "Careful," she'd growled. "I'm digesting a raccoon."

By the train tracks is where Dion saw the baby playing. It lay on its stomach, moving a diesel locomotive on the tracks. He was frightened of the baby, but he was lonely and had nobody to talk to since his father fell into a tub of F.D.&C. Red No. 40 food dye at the maraschino cherry factory. Since then, his mother was always at the casino with the man who'd replaced his chest with a mechanical bird cage. Dion had felt sorry for the house sparrows trapped inside.

"Hey," Dion said approaching the baby. "Want to see some drawings of my dog?"
The baby regarded Dion curiously. He crawled onto a patch of warm grass and gave a nod. They sat together looking at pictures of Dion's hound dog.

The baby soon fell asleep. It tossed its head in its dreams, and its eye movements too were so frequent, Dion thought they looked like eye storms.

At the sound of sirens, Dion slapped the baby's big toe to rouse him. "You better wake up, there's war happening," Dion said.

The baby's knees creaked as it steadied itself on its feet. It gurgled with joy and pointed up at a white rainbow that had just started to form between the morning fog.

A helicopter with its blades nearly touching the arc of the white rainbow hovered at a constant altitude over the fence. It made a circle around the baby, sent a stream of machine gun bullets meant to topple it to the ground. The baby reached its arms over its head and plucked the helicopter blades like daisies, grinding them into a thick powder.

Dion filled his pockets with broken helicopter pieces. "I've got huge pockets. I can fit lots of things in them," he said. From his right pocket he emptied a half-eaten apple, lifted it toward the baby. The baby gave the apple a hard eye, let out a series of bird sounds. Dion was sure the baby would make a good house sparrow. "It's alright," Dion said. "You have to look at the apple or else it'll rot."

The baby marched toward the city. Dion trailed at its bare feet. "You're like a kid brother to me now," he said. "I want to hear your tragic life story."

Radioactive Wolves

All my dreams take place in a house I've never been to.
A place west of the rubber trees where workmen plant fluorescent orange flags
on spots known to be flush with radioactive wolves.
My mother, inside, adjusts her wig, counts all her children.
She says, "The wolf pack spends all its life cycle circling the cord grass like someone in love." Then she leaves to huddle in a nearby culvert, and smoke cigarette after cigarette.
I have seven sisters, all named Wendy, each of them have their own separate dreams where they're cuddling a sleek black pony. They write to several government officials offering their services to charge into battle, ready to fight communism.
Our house has no roof. The sunlight breathes down, settles in among the furniture like a guest. Though they chew chunks of hair off our scalps, we often keep juvenile wolves strapped to our backs for warmth.
One of the Wendys says, "Things aren't so bad, are they? Creatures like this usually kill on fifty- three percent of their attacks. And we can still pray with our hands."
The truth is, I've never met a wolf I didn't like,
I've hated every job I've ever had. I once held a cricket,
its abdomen close to my ear,
and walked through a vein in its heart.

Crows

According to a study conducted by Cornell University,
New Caledonian crows are becoming more violent,
flapping wet wings at galactic cosmic rays so that the particles
travel down to press our hearts into cardiac arrest.
Take the situation upstate,
a number of crows were observed cawing loudly as they built their
own bomb in a laboratory.
They mixed hydrogen with other elements, then brought the small
explosive body to a forest of native pines.
They roosted around it,
hatching a metal egg churning with the fever of a meteor.
They chatted there for days.
Crow 1 shuffled his tail, said to Crow 2, "I found a dead clown
over by that brush."
Crow 2 responded, "Are you sure it was a clown? Seemed more
like an Elvis impersonator, what with the sequins and all."
"Perhaps," Crow 1 said. "Either way, I peeked inside its chest
cavity and everything in there was just small dogs and sandals."
"How many dogs were inside? Were they howling? I just hate
howling," Crow 2 said, a chill radiating through his black feathers.
Crow 1 thought for a moment. "I don't know. But there was music
coming from the chest walls. Very good music. I was so glad to
hear it."
Crow 3 was seen flying overhead with only one eye open, voicing
her dreams aloud.
"You know, I really can't wait to go to war," she said.

Song

"What's the source of all sound?" the man with a parasitic twin
brother on his chest asked the man with a bouquet of flowers for
a head.
They looked strong, and everything they knew they learned from
the horseflies and wild boars they kept hidden in the basement.
I wish I could say I dove under the table when I heard chronicles
of their wars,
but I laughed loudly and hissed.
The effects of a childhood disease left untreated, I explained.
The parasitic twin on the brother's chest kicked back the remains
of his beer.
He said, "The way I see it, one side of the brain controls the larynx,
then the babbling begins,
then the echoes,
the howling during cold days you spend alone with wolves.
But to talk over long distances, requires the formation of song,
the way a bird hears itself sing."
My father was the same way,
singing to himself, I thought.
Even when I was hoisted above his shoulders,
on our way to deliver illegal substances,
white powders he said made people feel like the happiest ponies
ever born.
The man with a bouquet of flowers for a head
married one of my father's ex-girlfriends.
I was the flower girl at their wedding.
During the toast
someone pulled a crank on the top of their head
to open a passage in the skull,
revealing an ocean inside,
a pod of dolphins leaping.

Robot

There's no season for hunting down giants,
but the hunt for robots changes seasonally.
Even the clickity-clackity sounds they make are creatures that
maintain their territory or else starve within hours.
I could head into robot country,
and tame a robot with its robot skeleton.
That's exactly what Stella did.
Taught her new pet the love of fire agriculture,
together burned down thickets to create open grassland where
wheat grains could grow abundant. Where to find a spot to dig for
clams is what I would have asked of it.
Better yet, train it to gently turn a fly's head 180 degrees and glue
it to the other side,
which would cause the god spirit in my middle ear to laugh with a
violence.
Might even make my head fall right off my shoulders.
In which case, I'd keep it in a cage and leave it outside,
so that it might attract crows to play with.
Lately, crows have been seen carrying their weight in their feathers,
swooping down for the likes of you or me
with gifts of jeweled sardines.
Piles of ruby fish eyes colliding like single-celled organisms
clustering to become
one moving barrier against the darkness.

Two Dreams

My dog had just been executed for witchcraft in front of our house,
then I wandered inside an opium den nestled somewhere in the
Arctic.
Other living things around me
flayed their arms about,
claimed they were trapped inside a salmon.
A salmon that had been brought up and raised by two giraffes
who were never happy at the same time
and who often stepped out
into afternoons blinded with light.
That was the first of two dreams.
In the other, we're at the wedding of the eight-legged girl our
brother had fallen in love with.
We called one of the extra legs Alice, after the black and white dog
of ours that had run away into a snowstorm and hadn't been seen
since.
Mostly, the bride looked bored and offered us plates of orange
food.
A fruit fly buzzed in my ear and whispered that he was a long-lost
ancestor.
"Everyone loves me," he said. "I've only been in one fight."

Island

The man marooned on a desert island
groomed a rock like a doll
to distract himself from
conversing with herring gulls.
He hadn't known any of them at all. They were drifters.
When he was a boy, he'd stayed awake for a lunar eclipse that
never materialized, and instead witnessed a ghost on the loose.
The ghost had been a drifter too.
It said it was looking for its body.
Last it'd seen it,
it was shivering uncontrollably,
likely dying of pneumonia.

The Horse

There was a horse loose in the hospital.
Really, he was more than a horse, he was like a father to us all.
He began by looking down our throats and arranging the scars
into neat piles.
Under the artificial lights, he fed bales of hay to the doctors and
ordered us to lick our wounds, as saliva starts your proteins to
unfold.
"When a glacier comes, it'll hold you to its chest for the next
5,300 years," he said galloping down the hall.
We didn't even mind if he stepped on our kidneys.
Though blindness was a potential side effect,
we thought of our near future in ice,
and the future after that.
Our lives as guerrillas carrying rifles in the mountains.
Before he left, we mined through the tiles in the Emergency
Room
looking for the remains of coconuts in the soil beneath.
Scent, when it's underground, takes on a color like hearts or
bones bleached by the sun.

Otters

I was on my way to school when two otters slunk out of the river,
wrapped their bodies around my right leg
and started chewing viciously.
I went to school with the otters inching closer to my femur
and I learned to love them. I called them Joe and Jane,
and they kept me company while satellites fell through the roof
of the cafeteria.
There was no clear explanation as to why
any of this was happening
or why all the girls in my history class had taken off riding atop
giant insects,
but I stayed behind and thought of all the things I might never
get to do,
like watch my dog become a baker or fashion myself a body out
of amber.
My ancestors would have looked for omens inside chicken livers,
but they died of cholera centuries ago.
Now I live in an apartment by myself
and the birds fly along the hearts of trees.
I can tell you more about the world.
This morning, sunlight fell onto my lap,
I cradled it for a moment
peeling back its particles,
its life
to look at the darkest places between the stars.

East Wind

The god of the east wind doesn't look like a god at all.
More rabbit than god,
more like a moon-white rabbit in a man-suit born
during a burst of evolution in the Cambrian period.
Soft as a blaze everything was back then, he says.
He puts an ice pack on his neck and asks if he can offer
assistance of a spiritual kind.

In this radioactive night, I practice the art of conversation.

All the joy, I tell him,
of the ragged peaks reaching the horizon, crystals engulfed
and gobbled up, the shapes of plants, tusks like a shovel, the
tiger prints on the ground, the claw muscle on the crayfish.
Did you ever think a girl criminal like me could learn to read the
expressions that ripple across the soul's faces?

That's when the god of the east wind slaps his rabbit hand against
his thigh and laughs.

He says the soul is made of bombs,
a bomb-soul stripping every piece of cotton out of soil, then
the plumes of radioactive snow, the tortoises clinging to roofs.
Best if you just sit here quietly,
watch something shiny take off in the distance after it leaves the
contents of its voice at your feet.

History

Neanderthals didn't have dogs.
Researchers say they carried branches like babies and sang to
them in two different voices.
Here it comes
that piece of sky with no night and no clouds above
a tribe of them consuming ancient forest moss.
We were making other plans at the time.
We floated on our backs with rocks on our stomachs to smash
invertebrates open.
Goats stormed to the south, and sure enough, we followed,
domesticating plants along the way.
Even today, the coconut trees sway over our sad houses.
They watch whenever a war goes on and off
or when large numbers of meteors crash down to turn us into
buckets of light.

Night

Our doll had come to life and grown nine feet tall.
She couldn't read, but all the same, she told us the day's headlines:
"One hundred and four children born in the new year. Two of
them with legs made entirely of palm leaves."
"Veterans of the last foreign war report hearing the voices of
mushroom clouds."
"Banana groves are rolling off their hills, leaving their roots face-
up to the sun."

She tucked us in
and we fell asleep,
though we feared she'd peck us open like a bun.

Outside, mosquitoes gathered under an open sky.
The dark sugarcane farmers wiped the sweat from their hands,
prayed for their ribcages to bloom into crystals.

Alligator

It was 1946. The war was over. The Russian scientists asked him if he remembered the bombing of the Berlin Zoological Garden and Aquarium. If he remembered hatching in Mississippi. If he remembered his mother. They repaired his improperly settled bones. Removed several of his decayed teeth. Prepared a fresh water habitat in a concrete enclosure. Brushed his arthritic tail. He'd been considered for the Russian space program. A seal-skin suit had been made to fit the whole 11.5 feet of him. He'd been rejected for space travel due to poor health. It was just as well, there was nothing an alligator could want on the moon. Two mixed breed street dogs were selected instead. The scientists fed them beef powder.

Of his origins, the following is known: On November 23, 1943, towards 8:00 PM, a direct bomb struck the Berlin Zoological Garden and Aquarium. The force flung the American alligator into the street. He then made his way through smoke and dust, past the scattered legs of four crocodiles, seven elephant tusks, and the horn of one black rhino. He stepped into the city in search of food and swamp and sunlight. He passed the thylacine, a marsupial carnivore that was confirmed as the last specimen of Thylacinus cynocephalus. She'd escaped the blaze of the Berlin Zoological Garden and Aquarium too, and was staring at the belly of a fallen airplane. The belly had fires and craters and within the craters more craters. Snow fell on the city for three years while the alligator sustained himself on a variety of small mammals. Periodically, he came in contact with humans, and he tried to eat those too. He learned to recognize the humans with uniforms and guns, and hid from them in black corners. The American alligator kept one eye open when he dozed, and once upon opening both eyes found a shivering woman throwing bread at his snout. She said words, but human words had no relevance to the alligator's world. He liked the bread, and through his larynx vocalized a low chorus of rumbles, which the woman rewarded with more bread.

It was the British who placed a rope around the alligator's neck. The alligator wrestled and spun on the ground. The British held him down as they tied his mouth shut. They'd won the war and gave the alligator to the Russians. The Russians put a sign up in front of his enclosure in the Moscow Zoo. It read Alligator mississippiensis. When scientists from the space program measured him for the seal-skin space suit, they told him if he were chosen, he'd see starlight up there that was once concentrated at the center of everything, but cornered and provoked to fight, it had no choice but to spread out like broad, scattered branches.

Mountain

A rarely seen occurrence like a jellyfish sitting in the half-light of
your living room
breathing shallowly through its cells,
its blue arms resting atop your grandfather's old nunchucks.
It's travelled long distances, it says, farther than it's ever been.
It belongs in someone else's home,
but asks for something new — a grilled cheese sandwich, something
fit for a human.
The whole thing makes you want to spit your gum out the window,
run through a forest
and past the rubber plantations
with a scream that has its own life.
The world we inhabit,
even now,
sends faint declarations of warning.
The eardrums develop a layer of hammered copper.
The shadows leave their houses.
Why would I be talking about the future?
It's the past that invades
like that ivy wrapping around the abandoned hotel on Fulton
Street.
But then again,
if I curl back into my body,
pull myself into a deep hug,
I can remember when the bacteria on my skin carried the scent of
mushrooms.
We were immigrants then, identical to the last major migration of
animals.
With no land of our own, I spent weeks sleeping in the back of
Sandra Castillo's car,
the rain clapping the roof awake then burying itself in the engine.
Open spaces became like thirst.
What it must feel like

to be a mountain,
to move rivers for those following the pulsing of navigation lights
north
to live on ice.

Peaches

We were on the grass in the back of the palace snacking on rare
songbirds when Jerónimo sprouted peaches out of his fingernails.
The peaches made him look large and threatening,
and in the early morning and dusk, he often used them to repel
insects and confuse predators.
Everyone felt safe and joyous. No one ventured into the badlands
anymore.
We had everything we wanted — taller, tougher grasses to digest,
and ceramic jars to store leaves.
When Jerónimo's heart suddenly stopped,
even the woman who'd turned into a cake
set aside the antelope's pink stomach she'd been hoarding away in
a shallow pit for winter,
and filled the uncooled air with mournful calls.
We grieved our friend's passing.
He'd never grow old enough to fall in love with a lady iguana as
he'd always wanted.
But we adapted to life without him. We rooted for tubers among
the land mines we were too light to trigger.
We honored all the gods and soon everyone was feeling romantic
again.
I was even thinking about being a better animal.
The good things I could become.
I could be the oracle sitting at the windowsill
looking into the past and future.
I saw us 6000 years ago in Dereivka
with our small, low crowned teeth, domesticated among all these
fragments.
And towards the future, I saw Beto's mother walk down the street
naked.
She'll carry a machine gun strapped to her back,
threaten us with launched bullets right through the retinas, but
we'll give her a sickly kitten to carry instead.
She'll thank us and say, "All these places are ugly anyway."

Stone Age

I was hell-bent on inhabiting a place where grass-
eating monkeys spent most of their day on the ground.
You see, my sleep-wake cycle was governed by the idea that
I would be the one to guide them into their own Stone Age.
I used magnetic fields to orient myself toward their location.
The sun above, my compass.
Along the journey, eagles captured in their beaks the warm air
within the dangerous places, warm air as big as dinner plates.
They wanted to possess something gorgeous, just as I did.
It was like a dream, and the last dream I'd had, I set a lighter to gasoline
in a hair salon.
The scissors cut bolts of fire after.
It made sense at the time. I mean, both my parents were hairdressers.
My father could draw well. My mother liked to shoot street cats
I'd wanted to be anything but human.
An oversized beast with glittering feathers on the throat would have
sufficed.
My mother slapped me for my stupidity, said she'd stash
me in an ash cloud if I ever said anything like that again.
I was relieved when she was eaten by Mrs. Winston's tiger.
That tiger locked in the apartment with a window overlooking the
135th street projects.
Even I witnessed his escape.
With a robust lower jaw, he devoured my mother's body slowly from
the outside in.
You, who've watched the snow cover the bodies of honey locust
trees, you must have known the tiger's head was full of jungle,
of claws gradually rising over the wild pigs running into the shadows
below.
Notice the stripes grown on your skin
and the sound that's become a current beneath.
I felt this longing too,
so I brushed my cheek against the moss blanketing the floor by a felled
tree stump and waited for the ground to sing.

Cosmonauts

The day of the cane toad's birthday,
I found a John F. Kennedy bust in the abandoned bakery.
I gifted it to him and it served him well as a spot to sit
and call out to one of his own in the humid evenings.
Though, there were silent parts between his calls
that made you look to the glow of the rocket ship
carrying the cosmonauts fleeing the plague.
No one knew what to do about the illness crawling the air out of
the lungs.
Still, I set my ctenophore trap and caught a no-name species of
free-floating comb jellies.
Brought to the surface, their cilia felt like an icy comet's leftovers,
like touching the trail of stones and ice that lingered.
They scattered along their tentacles flashes of blue, flashes of green.
They didn't like it here, didn't like the dogs scurrying,
the shadows hatched by the sea grape leaves.
So, off they went.
I only meant to look at them for a short while,
to tell them the grief that lived inside the attic of my inner ear,
the language I would use,
if only I knew the words.

Geniuses

There was a unicorn across the street
who ate a bomb and blew up.
I walked on his body,
the round back.
Felt the memory of the tremor through my feet.

I began to laugh, a hysterical laugh, as often happens when I'm
embraced by fear.

I covered the remains in sequins, so that Yamilis would see them
on her way back
and offer her respects.

The day had just started. My hair was covered in pollen.

When Yamilis arrived, she was in tears, expelled air harshly through
the mouth. She loved unicorns.
"At least nothing was rotting in the heat yet," she said.
"He had a history of heart trouble," I said. "Even before any of
this happened."

Our grandfather had raised unicorns as a boy. In the kitchen we
heard him say that cabbage soup includes an efficient conversion
of stored carbohydrates to sugars.
"It'll give you a jaw lined with fox teeth," he said. "Echolocation
develops after the first bite. You girls will be geniuses."

Evolution

In fact, it's lizards, not snakes, who've evolved to live inside discarded refrigerators.

And regeneration was mastered by the dinosaurs after fire and stone fell,

herded down from the holes in the universe.

Dig down into the soil and you'll find layers of their hearts.

When they shed their last bits of skin to become the whale,

they dipped into the water, tilted their heads,

and grew accustomed to the slow motion of the waves. And as for their legs,

in the intersection between birth and decay, they walked along the ocean floor.

All that humans could explain is that every

body aches, its cracks open.

Beneath the canopy, its new skin screams with thirst.

The way an organism feeds itself on whole sections of forest,

then itself becomes a bean field under the horizon.

Somewhere, a silverback gorilla caresses the wrinkles on his face and listens to the wind shake the leaves left to decompose on the ground,

the air passing through his windpipe, his vocal folds vibrating.

The average speed of light pressed against your pulse.

Rabbit

My dog, Ingu, had dug up a live two-headed rabbit from under the house and dropped it on my lap like a gift.

One head talked about his dreams of being a rice farmer. "I'd live in a valley and the valley would be like a green carpet when the rice grows in the patties."

The other head explained the process of thermal expansion. "The sea levels rise. The sawgrass retreats, water comes at us from all sides."

I fed the rabbit slivers of carrots straight from my hand.
Sometimes, after feeding,
each head would remind me that the fuel needed
to make a star and keep it running
is burning away.
And that soon
fish will burst out of the oceans,
fly through the windows.
The neighbors will wrap wet towels over their scales. They'll treat them like human beings,
often singing to them at night.

Extinct

When I picture extinct things, I put an x on their eyes,
on what their eyes had been.
The way to know they're dead,
not moved away to one lonely house.

I put an invertebrate coat on.
What it's made of, the edges of cells,
crawl spaces next to the rest of the fire
or a swallowed night with a gold-embellished beak.

In some invertebrates, memory can survive metamorphosis.
Look at the memories carried by extinct things driving for as long
as they're hungry.
This is the romantic part:
Extinct things that were alive in front of each another, took turns
braving danger at the front, blew kisses above decaying fruit.

The hibernating rodent learned to run from the predator that we
are during our arrival in North America.
Time traveler that I am, I see it all.
Back there, I'm a farmer. I fertilize the fields with the ancestors of
lobsters.

There are moments when I miss Coca Cola, miss yielding a
machinist's hammer,
but to think, I could have been lost along the way.
I've feared becoming lost as I'm chased through walls,
or worse still,
the loss of my herd,
their throats shaped
like the inside of a moon.

Bird

I saw a hen with my brother's face on it.

"What are you doing with those wings?" I asked him.

He clucked in a mix of hen-boy language. It was difficult to understand him, but he was family after all.

At first, he watched the hens and their rules. He watched how the other hens looked and how they moved around and how they picked food up with their beaks.

"I'm really getting the hang of this," is what I think he said.

There was another hen, a pretty one with black and brown feathers, that I think was his wife. He brought her things like rice and frogs. When I was with my brother and his wife, I spent a lot of time daydreaming

what if would be like to be a bird — not a hen like my brother, but maybe a starling with a machete strapped to a leg.

When rich people would come to the house, I could show them the machete and take their diamonds. They'd be scared and confused and mesmerized the whole time.

They'd go back to their own houses and a thousand more houses and tell the story of me. But in their story I'm not one, but a thousand more starlings, a mass of swooping wings diving to make the one supreme starling.

"They were really something," the rich people would say all wide-eyed. Then they'd get so tired, they'd want to prepare pillows and blankets and ready themselves to dream of the one supreme starling.

Everything #2

It was Wanda Reyes who'd trained the black hole to walk on a leash.

"I got it from some white family in Macon," she said. "I'm teaching it to talk, but all the sounds hurt its throat."

"Can it do anything exotic?" I asked.

Wanda rubbed her hands together excitedly, "Just watch," she said. She turned on the overhead light, and the black hole walled us in against the shadows of four clouds it quickly shred to bits.

A herd of zebras gathered around the back of Wanda's house, drawn there by the gravitational pull of the black hole.

Genetic analysis determined that the zebras were a subspecies of the Forested Plains zebra — a population that split from the evolutionary line when they began eating radioactive grasses.

Red oat grass flowers in full sunlight. The grass migrates and multiplies in the cells of the soil's airway.

The Abbot's robber frog, Eleutherodactylus abbotti, became the most striking of apex predators. They migrated here under a sparkling cloak of stars.

I had swallowed a yellow-eared parrot, or the yellow-eared parrot had swallowed me, I can't remember which. We flew into a bare room, save for the mountain gorillas chewing on wild celery. The gorillas coughed politely and asked our names and all the things we liked to do. We told them our names and all the things we liked to do and all the stars we'd seen form from gas and dust in the galaxy's outer arms and all the ones we'd seen shed their layers of hydrogen and gone supernova.

At the North American Mammal Museum, Araceli befriended a fortune teller who'd sailed on a cruise ship across several stellar nurseries. The fortune teller placed a warm hand on Araceli's forehead, she said, "You'll perform a long list of marvels. You'll carry a sword. Mushrooms will grow in your veins. Gills will protrude from the back of your neck."
But Araceli was only interested in finding her sister who'd caught an illness that turned her into an eastern coyote. She was last seen chasing a lamb down the highway.
"She's 1.9 feet tall and very grey," she said. "Can you see her killing lambs?"

I was fond of aquatic mammals. I taught an aquatic horse to swim to the left when I whistled. The dark mare swum to the surface of the pool and nudged her snout at my hands, nipped at my sleeves. She'd liked the sun on her face.

That row of trees pulled their rooted legs from under their bodies and turned their leaves toward the whistling of space junk passing overhead. The yellow-eared parrots sitting on their branches were responsible for interpreting the sounds of interstellar space.

Most of the South American megafauna survived the ice age. The mammoths, especially, had made the thousands and thousands miles trek south, following the above-ground roots and the dancing bees.

Agu took great pride in combing his young mammoth's fur coat. The mammoth rested his trunk inside his mouth, so that he looked like a baby sucking his thumb. Agu kept the light in the home he constructed out of cement and wood so low only the mammoth's silhouette could be seen.

Next door, the Minotaur shook rocks off his shoulders. He and Agu would spend their days together drinking Presidentes and playing dominos under the tropic sun.

The Minotaur often left half-eaten soldier skeletons covered in red geraniums and honeysuckle. When he was young, he'd fallen for a former beauty queen.
"A woman who could never return my love," he said. She'd slipped off a fishing boat in the middle of the night trying to bend a pipe in place.
"She's still down there," he said. "In a large, well-chilled house, happy being alone."

I hunted in a galaxy cluster known as Abell 2261. My black hole lived there, though it had gone silent.
"Have you run out of food to eat?" I asked it.
I fed it the beaks of several giant squids, but it never said a word.

The old dictator was famous for his cruelty, the mermaids knew this.
"He had built-in cheek pouches to store children for later consumption," one of the mermaids explained.
"I saw him kill three little boys," another mermaid growled from a corner. "All the boys did was steal a clock!"
"He'd been watching us," a child mermaid said. "He changed the shape of his eyeballs and watched us. We didn't like that."
When the seven human men dropped the old dictator over the cliff, into the dark, the mermaids grabbed him by the tail, pulled

him deep to where the water shudders. They tore right through to get at the heart, the familiar rhythm of the heart, to lock his pulse in silence.

In the bodega on Mermaid Avenue, I spread gold dust over the cans of spaghetti. I dusted the tan and white bodega cat and the votive candles of Chango Macho the Great Spirit of Good Luck. The bodega cat purred, and a golden glow enveloped us like dusk over a mangrove swamp.

Acknowledgements

Grateful acknowledgement is made to the following publications, in which many of these poems first appeared: The Yale Review ("Animal Kingdom," "Axolotl,"); Guernica ("River"); Poetry Northwest ("Stories"); The Antioch Review ("Rabbit"); Quarterly West ("Mollusk"); Fugue ("Radioactive Wolves"); PRISM international ("Winged Insects"); North American Review ("Night"); Mid- American Review ("The Food Chain"); Poetry South ("Two Dreams"); The Bitter Oleander ("Bad News," "Evolution"); Poet Lore ("Mountain"); The Moth ("Beasts"); storySouth ("Otters"); Grub Street ("Girls"); The Cincinnati Review ("Queen"); The Idaho Review ("Moth," "Mermaid," "The Pulmonary System."); Salamander ("Biologies," "Peaches"); The Poetry Review ("Song"), Fence ("White Rainbow"); Gulf Coast (Minotaur)

About the Amy Roa

Amy Roa is a Dominican American poet and naturalist. She is the author of Radioactive Wolves (Steel Toe Books, 2023) winner of the 2021 Steel Toe Books Poetry Award. Her poems have appeared in *The Yale Review*, *The Cincinnati Review*, *Gulf Coast*, *The Idaho Review*, and elsewhere. She lives in Brooklyn, New York.

CPSIA information can be obtained
at www.ICGtesting.com
Printed in the USA
JSHW010320101122
32867JS00003BA/271

9 781949 540376